EVERYDAY STEM

FRICTION

Joanne Mattern and John Willis

AV2
www.av2books.com

Step 1
Go to **www.av2books.com**

Step 2
Enter this unique code

ZPYIUTJLP

Step 3
Explore your interactive eBook!

AV2 is optimized for use on any device

Your interactive eBook comes with...

Contents
Browse a live contents page to easily navigate through resources

Audio
Listen to sections of the book read aloud

Videos
Watch informative video clips

Weblinks
Gain additional information for research

Try This!
Complete activities and hands-on experiments

Key Words
Study vocabulary, and complete a matching word activity

Quizzes
Test your knowledge

Slideshows
View images and captions

... and much, much more!

EVERYDAY STEM

FRICTION

CONTENTS

CHAPTER ONE

Slow Down!

Nikki straps on her helmet and steps onto her skateboard. She pushes off with her foot. At first, she rolls along quickly. Soon, however, she starts to slow down.

The skateboard's wheels are attached to **axles**. The skateboard slows down partly because of the friction between the wheels and the axles. Friction happens when two objects rub against each other.

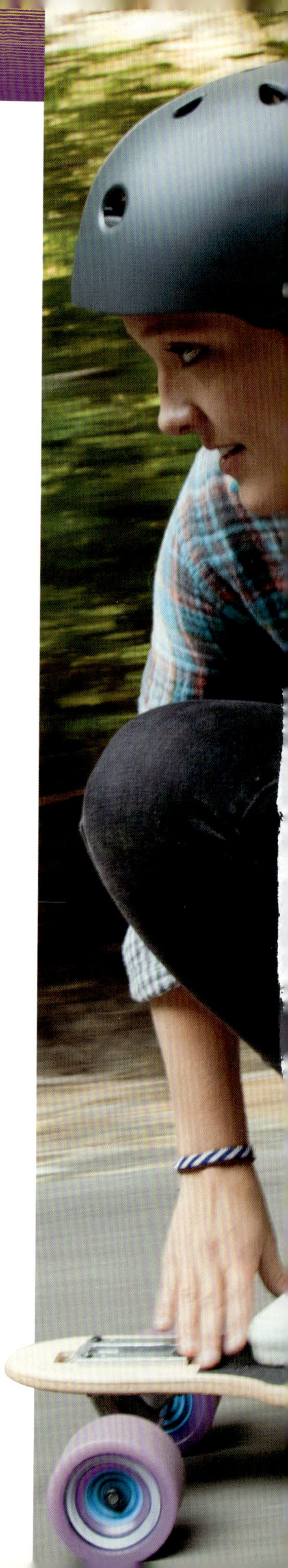

Once again, Nikki pushes against the street with her foot. Her skateboard starts to roll faster. She is moving quickly when she sees her friend Andrew. She wants to stop and talk to him. Nikki puts down her foot. She drags it against the street.

The skateboard slows. Nikki uses the friction of her shoe against the street. The friction slows her skateboard. Now she can talk to her friend.

The friction between the shoe and the ground helps a skateboarder slow down.

Ice skates move easily across ice because they create very little friction.

We use friction every day. Without friction, things would slide around all the time. Friction helps people in many ways. Sometimes, people look for ways to create more friction. Other times, they need ways to create less. In both cases, friction is an important part of our lives.

CHAPTER TWO

What Is Friction?

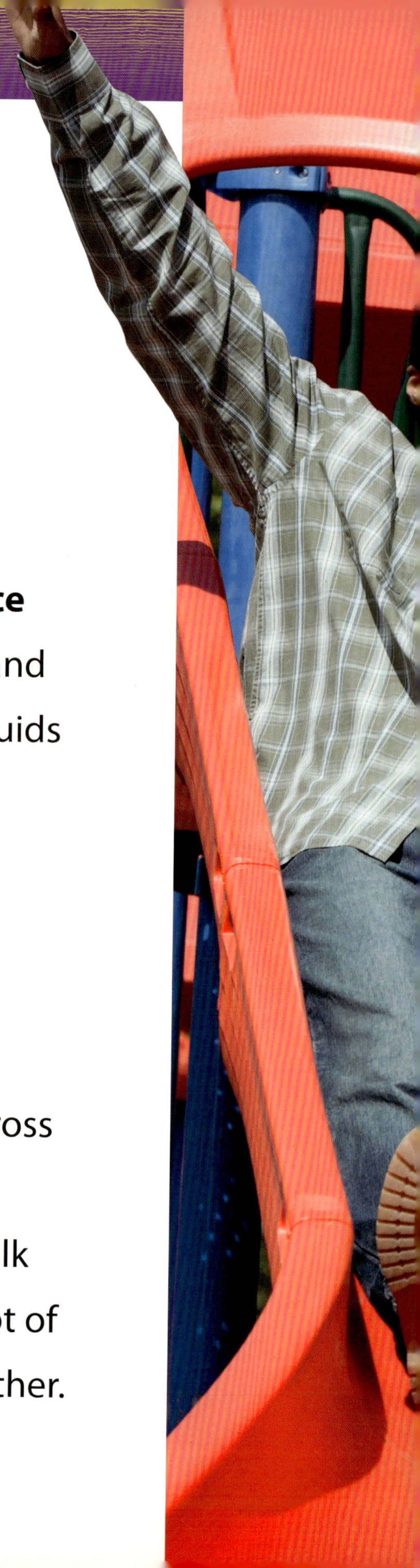

Friction happens when one **substance** rubs against another. Solids, liquids, and gases all create friction. Friction in liquids and gases is known as resistance.

Some objects create more friction than others. Rough objects create the most friction.

Suppose you are sliding a big rock across the sidewalk. It is hard to do. That is because the rock is rough. The sidewalk is rough, too. These objects create a lot of friction when they rub against each other.

When you swim, there is friction between you and the water.

Some objects are smooth. Imagine being on ice. It is hard to start moving. Once you start, however, it is hard to stop. That is because the ice is smooth. It does not create a lot of friction against your shoes.

Many liquids **reduce** friction. They can make things slippery. If you walk across a wet floor, your feet might slip. That happens because the water reduces the friction between your feet and the floor.

A moving object has energy. When friction slows down a moving object, that energy causes the temperature to increase. If you rub your hands together very firmly, they will soon start to feel warm. That is because the friction between your hands causes them to get hotter.

Friction can also cause an object to get a static charge. This happens when objects rub against one another. **Electrons** are tiny charged particles. They pass from one object to the other. Imagine walking across a carpet and touching a metal doorknob. You may get a shock. Electrons from the carpet jump between you and the metal.

HOW FRICTION WORKS

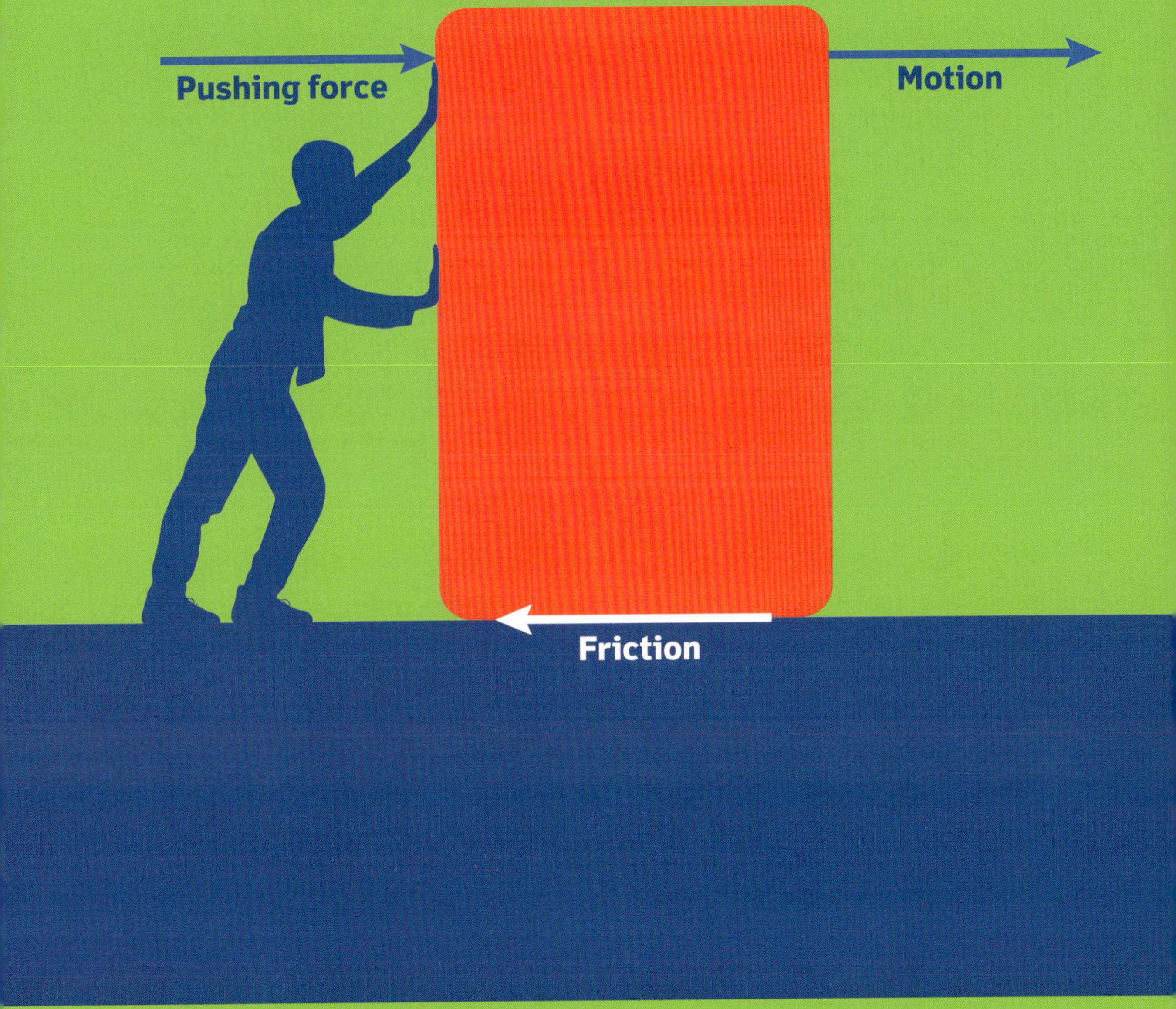

Friction happens when you push an object across a surface.

Wheels are used in many everyday objects to reduce friction.

Friction can be helpful in many ways. For instance, friction helps us slow down when we want to stop. Without friction, we would slip and slide whenever we tried to walk around.

Sometimes, we need to create less friction. One way to reduce the effects of friction is by using wheels.

It is usually easier to move a heavy box if you put it on a wagon, for example. The friction of the rolling wheels is usually less of a problem than the friction of the box sliding along the ground.

Liquids can also help reduce friction. Adding water or oil usually makes it easier for objects to slide and move.

Think about a squeaky door. It may be difficult to close. When you put oil on the **hinge**, however, the door closes more easily. That is because the oil reduces the friction at the hinge.

Oil reduces friction between the parts of a bike chain.

CHAPTER THREE

Friction in Our World

Friction happens in many ways. It happens whenever we move. Suppose you are riding a bike. When you use the **brakes**, they rub against the wheel. This causes the wheel to turn more slowly. The bike also slows down because of the friction between the wheels and the road.

Car engines would get too hot without oil.

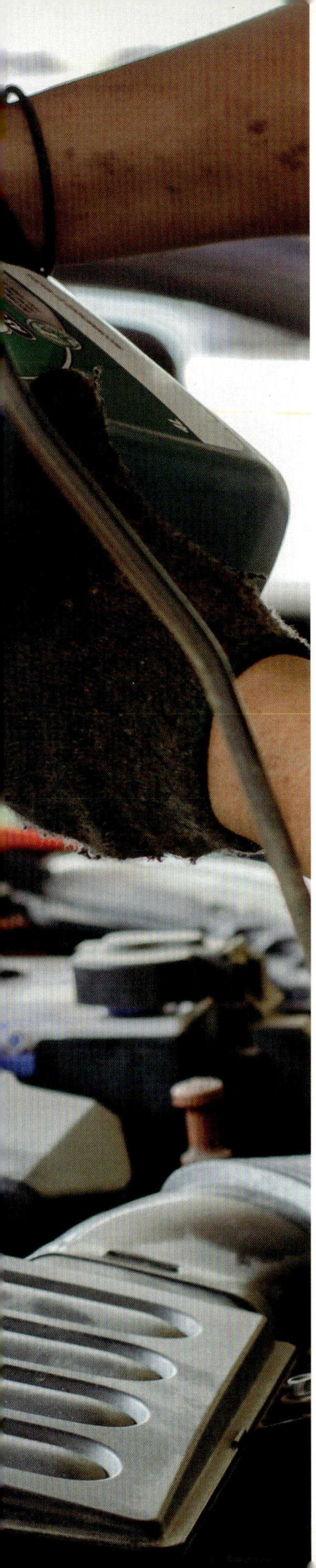

Friction also happens when parts of a machine rub together. This can be bad because it causes the parts to get hot. The parts can also wear away or break. To **prevent** this, people put oil on some machines. It helps the parts move more smoothly. For example, a car engine has many moving parts. Oil helps reduce the friction. It keeps the engine cooler.

Water slides have low friction. That is because water is a liquid that has low friction. It makes people move quickly down the slide. If the slides did not have water, people would go much slower. Water reduces the friction between the body and the slide.

The **atmosphere** around Earth is made of gases. When a rocket moves through the gases, it experiences friction. That friction causes the rocket to get very hot. For this reason, rockets are covered with special tiles. They protect the rocket from getting too hot.

Friction is part of our world in many ways. Whenever you move or slip, think about how friction is acting on your body!

When scientists design rockets, they must think about friction.

Creating Friction

Does an object experience more friction on some surfaces than on others? Do this experiment to find out.

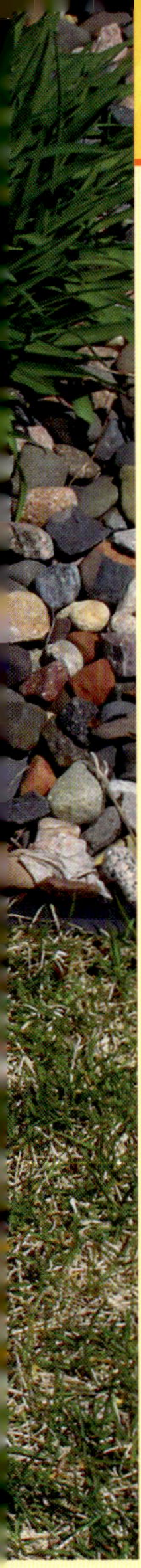

STEP 1 Get a wooden board. It should be about 3 feet (0.9 metres) long and 1 foot (0.3 m) wide. Cover one side of the board with sandpaper.

STEP 2 Make sure the sandpaper side is facing up. Lift one end of the board to create a ramp.

STEP 3 Place a book at the top of the ramp. Let go of the book. If the book does not slide, make the ramp steeper. See how quickly the book slides down.

STEP 4 Flip the board over so that the smooth side is facing up. Keep the ramp at the same angle.

STEP 5 Place the book at the top of the ramp. Let go of the book. See how quickly the book slides down this time. Which surface creates more friction on the book? How could you make the book slide even faster?

THE FRICTION QUIZ

- 1 -

When does friction happen?

A. When two objects rub against each other

- 2 -

What would happen without friction?

A. Things would slide around

- 3 -

What is friction in gases and liquids called?

A. Resistance

- 4 -

Why do ice skates move easily over ice?

A. Skates create very little friction on ice

- 5 -

Do rough or smooth objects have more friction?

A. Rough

- 6 -

Does a water slide have more or less friction than a dry slide?

A. Less

- 7 -

Why is a wet floor slippery?

A. Water reduces friction

- 8 -

Which parts of a bike use friction to stop?

A. Brakes

- 9 -

What liquid is often used to help the parts of a machine move more smoothly?

A. Oil

- 10 -

How does friction affect a rocket?

A. It makes it very hot

Key Words

atmosphere: gases that surround a planet

axles: bars that wheels spin on

brakes: parts of a vehicle designed to help it stop or keep it stopped

electrons: charged particles that can be in atoms or on their own

hinge: an object that connects a door to a wall and allows the door to open

prevent: to stop something from happening

reduce: to make less

substance: any type of material, such as a solid, liquid, or gas

Index

Published by AV2
14 Penn Plaza, 9th Floor New York, NY 10122
Website: www.av2books.com

Library of Congress Control Number: 2020936965

ISBN 978-1-7911-2372-7 (hardcover)
ISBN 978-1-7911-2373-4 (softcover)
ISBN 978-1-7911-2374-1 (multi-user eBook)
ISBN 978-1-7911-2375-8 (single-user eBook)

Printed in Guangzhou, China
1 2 3 4 5 6 7 8 9 0 24 23 22 21 20

052020
101319

Designer: Terry Paulhus Project Coordinator: Priyanka Das

Every reasonable effort has been made to trace ownership and to obtain permission to reprint copyright material. The publisher would be pleased to have any errors or omissions brought to its attention so that they may be corrected in subsequent printings.

The publisher acknowledges Getty Images, iStock, and Shutterstock as its primary image suppliers for this title.

First published by Focus Readers in 2018.